A Marshy Pond

Philippe R Hebert

Table of contents

A cloudy and misty day

At the pond center
a mound exists and upon which
a deciduous pine thrives
having existed perhaps a hundred years
all twisted and gnarled
and at the marshy edge
where minnows, tadpoles, and frogs gather
there stands the egret

The egret hunter
almost as patient and rooted
as the pine

It preens itself
after a meal of minnows and tadpoles
the rocks and lily pads
are undisturbed
and only small ripples on the water

No wildlife
approaches the water
reeds, cat-tails, or marsh grasses
as the rain and mist has driven
all to their beds
except a small brown wren.

The Marshy Pond

The small pond bathed in moonlight
shades of yellow and white
with the edges in dark brown.
Who knows how long the egret
has been standing there motionless

So still that he appears
to be part of the scene
but that was the egrets plan.
A spider skates over the water
causing the tiniest of ripples.

The minnows pectoral fins quiver
keeping it in its place
while the frog keeps one eye
on a nearby fly.

A Meandering Brook

A meandering brook
through a glen
a grove of trees on the left
and an open meadow
on the right.

At the edges of the water
is a marshy area
alive with critters
of all sorts
both large and small.

Tadpoles, frogs, and mosquitoes
all feed the fish and the egrets
The fish, in turn,
feed man
and man…well…man…just is.

The air is crisp and clean
even though the temperature is mild.
It's like what the air is
immediately following
a rain storm.

The Heron

A white heron at water's edge
stark against the dark outline
of the woods in the background
and reflected onto the pond's stillness
by the setting sun

The heron doesn't recognize
the beauty it's created
in just existing
and searching
for frogs and minnows

Picturesque as in a Japanese Shoji screen
contrasting yellows, black brown, grays, and white
delicate in its entirety
with one bare stoic tree in the background
standing alone in spite of natures brutality.

Two white cranes stand motionless
against the same background of darkening woods
hunting food and posing for another shoji screen.

The image, sharply defined in the twilight
and reflected on the water's edge.
The sky is tinted shades of yellow and gray
as if forecasting happiness and good fortune.

A thirsty doe leads a small herd
slowly and cautiously approaching
the need for water and the lush grasses
overcomes their inherent fears.

How peaceful it all seems

A Daffodil

An old man sits alone at his desk
staring at the facing wall
that is covered in clippings
His ego wall, he calls it.
Poems and stories of bygone days
yesterdays flowers all wilted.

But in the far right corner
is an image
his favorite
a heron feeding at water's edge
dusk colors
black, gray, yellow, and white
are illuminated by the
light of a setting sun.

The old man's mind wanders
thinking of the past
then suddenly lurching
with thoughts of the now
It's 3 AM yet again
that's the routing
nodding off at 8PM and awake at 3AM.

After dressing a casual stroll outside at sunrise
a bright yellow daffodil catches his eye
unable to resist he snips it
and carefully pins it to the wall
directly front and center.

This makes his day.

An Arrangement

Can you see it ?
the arrangement !
from back to front

A clump of bamboo
half dozen hibiscus
bird of paradise

A fractured mahogany stump with
cymbidium orchards
smooth dark river rocks and moss

Why am I imagining
these beautiful arrangements
is death so near?

Bird of Paradise

Aptly named
only one look
the distinct design and color
says loud and clear
you are not of this earth

An ethereal beauty
orange, yellow, blue, or purple
a symbol of beauty and grace
or perhaps freedom
but doesn't survive shade

Dawn Over The Pond

Alone at dawn
at the edge of the pond
with the water and breeze still
the magnificence of nature all around.

Shadows and dark outlines
are all that can be seen
but one can hear the crickets and frogs
calling to their mates.

Why do I sit to look and listen?
What do I expect to see or hear?
It's simply for the time to recall
and ponder decisions made.

And to gaze at the waning moon
the shadow of the trees
and the heron already out
hunting for food.

How surreal the shadow
of a lone tree seems
The reflection of the moon on the water
and the mist rising off the pond

A solitary turtle paddling along
the contrast of the brilliant
white heron on the dark waters
how mesmerizing the sight

The brilliant white heron against the
dark shadows and the waters.

The branches of the trees
like arms upraised.

El Condor Pasa

Haunting and elegant the flute or the Quena
and how arresting the song about a giant bird
the Peruvian unofficial anthem
seemly a lofty tribute

El Condor Pasa enchanting
seemingly symbolizing freedom and love
but in reality it's about Peru's
mining, lost lives, and the brutal conditions

The Andean condor life span equals a mans
wing span over 10 feet
with regimes spread wide
featherless head it soars upwards of 20,000 feet

Traveling over 200 miles in the clouds
above the Andeans mountain
it appears to glide and soar forever
eating only carrion

El Condor Pasa commemorates
Exploitation, loss, and suffering
often played at funerals
appropriate for man and nature.

Hibiscus

Another tropical beauty
with a myriad of colors
scarlet, yellow, pink, violet
basking in the sun

The summer breeze
causes the hibiscus to sway
against dark green of leaves
like an invitation of sorts

Imaginings

My mind's abuzz
as I surround myself
with imaginings
of flowers and shrubs

I envision myself
sitting among clumps of bamboo
the wind stops
everything is quite

The sun warms
everything it touches
even the smooth dark rocks
seem to respond to the warmth

Moon Over The Ruined Castle

What night is this?
so grey dark and foggy
a ruined castle deep in the background.
Only the cries of a mountain cat exist.

A deciduous pine peers through the misty fog
leaving only a haunting melody.
The plaintive sounds of the most popular
Japanese folk song* ever.

As the moon recedes
and the sun's rays
begin to dissipate the fog and mist
the forlorn feeling persists.

The misery, pain, and death
still prevail, but less.
Clouds still hang low and
mask the valley below.

Only the cries of a mountain cat
is left to bear witness.

19

*Rene Paulo plays it
(Moon Over The Ruined Castle)
again and again as if on a loop.

A Mundane Life

Have you ever thought
about all the mundane things
in a day or a year
that make up a life?

Isn't that what a life is?
Just an iteration
of mundane things
strung together.

One day you're older
and then you're old
looking back
you wonder how it happened

The kids are grown
a working career is over
and suddenly
you're 70 or 80

What of significance
and meaningfulness
did you accomplish

Where…when
was that conscious thought
that passed for a life?

The Leaves

The leaves on the trees
appeared from one day to the next
naked bare branches
were suddenly transformed

No longer black shadows
against the dark brown sky
bare naked branches
housed wrens and squirrels

As the wind
pummeled the sprouting buds
unfurling the leaves
not yet ready to open

Small buds erupt
the ground is soon covered
the wind is merciless

Bare naked branches
now covered with a halo
of misty green

Spring has arrived.

Live In the Past

How we deceive ourselves
with thoughts of all sorts
health, fitness, attuned to the present
when, in fact, our cloistered self
allows the world to pass us by.

We think that we are as
agile and quick witted
but we live in the past
whatever we choose, whatever we like
is the familiar.

Old books, old music, old friends
hardly the ambiance for new thoughts
no, no we say!
we dissect the old, the past
so as to provide new thoughts.

Hardly rational !
but in our mind
we race against time
because time is now so limited

I'd like to share
what's taken me a lifetime
to learn, to assimilate
but no one wants to hear
the ramblings of an old man.

No, they say
you are outdated, get with the times
'cause you're "out to lunch".

You live in the past.

Carrying A Torch

Oh yes, I still carry a torch
for you even after all these years.
My soul shudders
and my heart beats faster
at the very thought of you.

It seems as if our relationship
was never concluded.
Who ever said,
if you burn hot you'll burn out
Never knew us.

Early mornings and late nights
the loons call out with their plaintiff songs,
only adding to my recollections of you
and the hollow feelings that exists
it's just a bit of the blues.

Mist Shrouding the Moon

Laying back
in the bottom of the canoe
letting the swells
lap at the canoe sides
making it sway slightly
and the sound
like gentle slaps on the wood.

How peaceful to gaze at
the stars and mist shrouding
the 3rd quarter moon.
The background sounds
of loons, frogs, and crickets
a cacophony of noise.

The breeze whiffs the intoxicating
scent of honeysuckle
it's all so mesmerizing
that the quarrels and vitriol
is dissipated and only
an empty hole remains.

A Texas Sky

The burnt orange Texas sky
so reminiscent of the tejas of old
that once glittered from
Fort Worth and San Antonio
to Mesilla and El Paso
exist now only sporadically.

The Blue Bonnets
no longer cover the hills,
valleys, and plains
even the cactus
have lost their strongholds.
The yellow rose is almost a memory.

I believe bougainvilleas and jacarandas abound
while chollas cactus and rocks
are the new state flower.

Texas of old is, dead indeed,
a faded memory as the wagon trains
and cattle drives.
Although some horse ranches continue
it's mostly dude ranches and
exotic animal hunting ranges.

Austin and Dallas is as cosmopolitan
as New York or LA
and populated by those same peoples.
for Texas of old visit San Antonio,
El Paso, or Amarillo
and good TexMex cooking is there as well.

Tejas

Burnt orange and red Spanish tile roofs,
correctly called tejas,
seems so mundane a topic
but as seen collectively as a pueblo
from a mountain top
they are quite picturesque,
especially when surrounded by lush green vegetation
with the many shades from dark green
of the forest trees
to the lightest pale green of the grasses.

Early morning's bright sunlight
enhances the colors and
the mist makes it all seem a dream
but the cook fires
portends a hearty breakfast
of refried beans, eggs, tortillas, and coffee
because the workdays are long
with only a small block
of dried smoked cheese and tortillas for lunch.

Sometimes, when there's time
gnarled hands and stooped shoulders will put

a new edge on the machete
because basic tools must be maintained.

Late afternoon brings a pleasant relief
with a glass of beer and peanuts with friends.
Supper will call together the family
for grilled beef, beans, and rice.
Desert is typically a glass of cane rum and a cigar
over a game of dominos with neighbors.
Life is simple and only promises
another hard day's work just like yesterday.

Tolling of Bells

There is nothing these days
as dramatic as the tolling of bells
to draw attention to death
of one's friends

It seems as if death
sneaks in and passes by
without a whisper

Months pass by before we become
aware of someone's death.
How sad that events such as this
go unnoticed almost as if
they are of no consequence.

Relocate me to a casita
with my dog.
Rice and beans with a side of tortillas
and a block of queso auhmado cheese
I can survive and perhaps even thrive.

The Remembering

Reminiscing with a friend of over 40 years
brought forth good and pleasant memories
how wonderful it seemed
to recall yet another absent friend

We were the yoga teacher, the poet
and the fat cat.
A trio brought together
by the planning of our lives long, long ago

The association that evolved from acquaintances,
into colleagues, then friends
was all based on our unemployment
and the search for our future long ago

Now the thinning white and gray hair
the limp from surgery
the almost inability to stand and walk
without assistance just showed our octogenarian ages

Lives relived through
stories and words shared
soon melancholy sets in
matching the dreary rainy day mood

As we ate and drank as before
the ugly weather of March
was replaced by the warmth in the telling
It was the warmth of friendship

How the years floated away
the dreadful experiences of family matters
and the work issues, problems, and terminations

were dispelled by "just pay me and I'll move on"
although said in a cavalier manner the hurt was there

Regardless how we seemed unaffected
the lines around the eyes and
the tightening of the lips and set of the jaw
showed the pain and hurt of the past
it cannot be dismissed so easily

We casually planned a reunion of sorts
a road trip (or a pipe dream) emanating from
North Carolina, Maryland, and New Jersey
heading North by train

North to the Lac St Jean, but the destination was
unimportant,
visiting Saguenay, Chicoutimi, and Hébertville
and we know we can get fat cat to come along
with the promise of cigars and Lagavulin

But, in the end, it felt,
it seemed as if we had recovered
just by the telling
after all, we were more than just friends

**We had truly shared life
and at our age, how many more road trips can there
be?**

Retirement

So you want to retire
you feel used up
and want to rest and recharge.
That's fine…retire!
Rest, sleep, and laze about
Soon you'll see.

Soon you'll see
that retirement takes work
not everyone can take it.
To do nothing
to think nothing
soon you'll go a bit mad.

Soon you'll yearn
for some action
you'll want that old regimentation.
Soon you'll recall
that old camaraderie
soon you'll try to reconnect.

But your former colleagues
are all busy
that common thread is cut!
So now you're alone
now try the breakfast shop
try sitting at the liars table

But you don't fit there either
And TV's a bore
you can read only so much.
Soon you'll look

at the classifieds
soon you'll talk to recruiters

But they cant be bothered
you've cut that thread
you're alone.

And your wife doesn't want
your supervision
you're alone.

You are retired!

Get A Grip

As an octogenarian
with just a handful
of minutes left
memories of days of old
flood the mind.

Thinking of doing
things that are no longer
reasonable nor feasible.
Old man, get a grip
reality is at hand.

You shouldn't drive
unless it's a mobility scooter.
Let go of your fantasies
and try to focus
on reality.

What you can do
is no longer what you think
you can do
nor is it what you
should do.

Get a grip
swallow your pride
sit on your ass
write another line
but don't get carried away.

You're not going to amount
to anything at this late stage
publish another book
what's the point?
It just costs money.

We Managed

I've loved and won
you were in my heart
from the very first

Hardly a new romance
but I persisted
I won you at last

And within a year
I asked for your hand
despite a war we wed

This July we be weeded for 55 years
how time flies
'cause it seems like only yesterday

Your English was poor
my Spanish was nonexistent
but we managed

Yesterday I watched you
walk away
how small and thin
you are.

Where The Dahlias Grow

You said,
"I'll meet you where the dahlias grow"

A foot path
over a bridge

There is the field
awash with multi colored dahlias

You are not there
but I'll wait among the dahlias

But the dahlias say
you wait in vain.

Willow in the Wind

As the light fades
from her eyes
And the cinnamon color of her skin
turns yellow
I think back over the years
and wonder what became of the time.
The volatility has slowly vaporized.
It seems like only yesterday
that we were young
It seems like yesterday
that we existed
only for each other.

Her eyes held only love and admiration
mine held only devotion and adoration for
the young brown girl I held.
She was so petite and delicate
that it seemed a squeeze
would break her
But 55 years have passed
and I love her all the more.
So tiny, petite, and delicate
but she wont break
she will bend like the
willow in the wind.

How can I go on
without my lover,
my partner,
my best friend?
Time has lead us
to this fork
she'll tread one path
and I will live alone on another.

We will talk as before
but only in my mind.
Go softly, my willow in the wind
And I'll stay here alone.

Fussa Japan

In the dead of winter
entering a small village in mid afternoon
dark brown wood buildings hug the narrow street

Some buildings have cloth banners fluttering in the wind
the banners are emblazoned with Japanese characters
one banner also has a picture of a bottle of beer

Entering and greeted by an old man bowing
with an open sweeping arm he invites us in
in spite of the cold outside there is a warm glow within

The walls are all hand hued boards
the tables and benches are of the same material
the rooms are divided by colorful strips of cotton

Not even 25 years since the occupation
our host must have somewhat intimidated by our
presence
forging ahead and sitting at a table towards the back

Ordering Karin beer and selecting chicken teriyaki
this obviously pleases the old man
assembling the food and placing onto a hibachi ten at a
time

Bits of chicken do not slake our appetite
consuming probably more within half an hour
than he's sold all week

The snow has started to fall as darkness sets in
we remain and continue to drink more beer
the old man is obviously concerned that we couldn't pay

Placing a pile of Yen and MPC on the table
gesturing for the old man to come and take payment
he roots through the pile taking a few bills

He smiles and bows deeply several times
We nod and bow in return
but order more food and beer

Now with a foot of snow
we trek down an alley
into a Japanese only hotel

Leaving shoes at the door
we are greeted with bows ad shown into rooms
girls come and strip off our clothes

Now in kimonos, led into communal baths
stripped and lathered with soap
rinsed off now into the pools

Water intended to cook lobsters
relaxed muscles and evaporate the alcohol
while we watch the snow

New kimonos and into bed
piled high with 4 or 5 quilts
so heavy, cant move

Uninterrupted sleep
this wont be
once and done.

SOME DAY

Sitting on the patio of my old adobe house
in a pueblo high atop a mountain.
Morning has yet to shed its light.

It's cool and a bit foggy,
a mountain cat calls and a dog barks
almost as if answering.
Steaming rich black coffee in hand
ready to meet the new day.

What will be encountered?
What shall we do?

Just put off everything for now
and light the first
cigar of the day.
See the blue gray cloud of smoke
and smell the pungent sweet aroma.

Now just lean back and
enjoy the coffee and cigar
life will take care of itself for now.

The leaving of the cities
and simply being "in the moment"
is harder than you think.
But then again it's wonderful to simply
exist in this heaven I've created.

We can think and write later today…
perhaps in the cantina
or under the old tree in the plaza.

But no rush… it will be
there tomorrow too.

So many words float about
some landing on a page.
Maybe it will be this blue smudge
that nobody will read.
But that's ok maybe – someday.

The Night Comes Quickly

The night comes quickly
and then the sounds
seem to be amplified.
Sitting on the patio
alone with my thoughts.

I can't help but wonder
what did I accomplish?
have I achieved anything?
did I make a difference today?
Is the world a better place?

Reading sometimes breeds inspiration
so, jotting down words which are
conscripted for future use,
images appear and some vaporize
while others remain.

Paint those images with words,
splash them on the page
return later to refine them
but it's enough now
to capture them as if they might float away.

But for now
the night gobbles up the inspiration
leaving no telltale sign
that anything occurred
just a blank page.

Thunder and Lighting

The light rain turns
into a deluge
the kind of rainstorm that can
only be experienced in the summer

Sheets of rain
beat into the ground as lightning flashes
creating gullies
that quickly fill with rain water

Water runs off the roof through a water spout
and shoots 20 feet into the air
before the arc begins to drop
splashing across the sodden earth

How awesome the storm
but leaving the air clean
and sweet smelling
as if a baptism cleansed the earth

Black Lake Waters

Waters of the lake
black with tannins
not only sustain
aquatic life but
all animals surrounding

Pines and spruce trees
hug the shore line
ducks, geese, and loons
yonder laze about
droppings feed the fish

At night bats swoop down
to eat bugs and mosquitoes
meanwhile loons plaintiff call
crickets and frogs croak on the shore
deer and lesser animals venture forth

A hawk swoops down and
feeds on a rabbit
Quail and partridge roost nearby
tiz a microcosm of life

Out of My Memories

Out of my memories
the unbidden came
of my tribe of
1st Nation People
we lived in the Northern sections.

Later these were called Provinces
of Quebec and the Lac St Jean
and still later the States some say New England
the winters long
and the summers short.

But the land was bountiful
with every manner of game
and even more fish
We were rarely hungry
and the 1st People multiplied.

As a youngster
we would run and at play
we would mimic our elders
hunting, tracking, and wrestling
these were things we would do as adults too

We also tended to the horses,
made flaming arrows from cat-tails
smoked dried reeds
made and drank sassafras tea
that was my favorite
because of the root beer like smell

Bio

Philippe R Hebert is an 80 year old poet, writer, and story teller.

- Book of Vietnam War poems "Elephant Ears and Bamboo Shoots" published by Human Error Publishing
- Poetry Book "A Begging Bowl" to be published in 2024 with Human Error Publishing
- Poetry Chapbook in manuscript form "A Saffron Robe" with Human Error Publishing
- "A Shoji Screen" with Cyberwit Publishing
- "A Marshy Pond" with Cyberwit Publishing
- "A Safron Robe" with Cyberwit Publishing
- Selected for inclusion in the Summer Anthology "Bards Poetry Review 2024"
- Pushcart nominee
- Exit 13 Issue, #29 publish "Tejas"
- Canyon Voices "The Heron" & "The Night Comes Quickly"
- Vietnam War Poetry December 2022 4 poems, April 2024 2 poems
- Spill Words Press January 2023, May 2023, August 2023
- Published in The Stillwater Review 2023
- Arts By The People December 2023
- Anthologies "The More I Forget" 2022, & "Nature Knows the Way" 2023
- Poetry Nation "Peace & Serenity" & "Retrospectively"
- Handbook for Savings in Freight & Logistics
- Working on a book for children titled "Fritz, My Bestest Friend"
- Over 60 Manufacturing Publications
- A Case Study at Lehigh University

- ☐ Active member of Newton NJ Writers Roundtable
- ☐ Active member of Poetry At The Barn
- ☐ Active member of Newton NJ Library writers and Poets

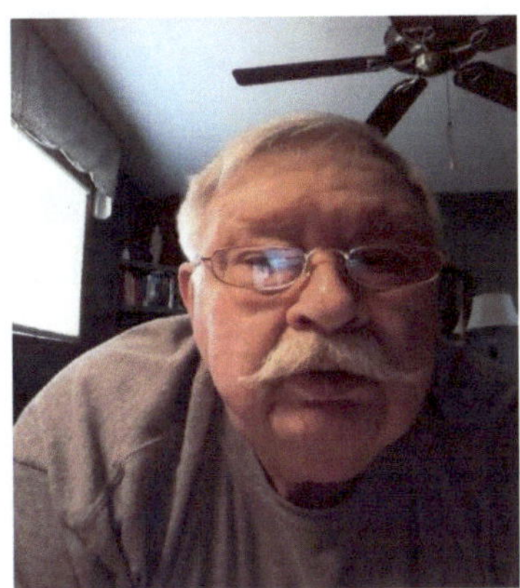